Practice Notes

This Journal Belongs To:

_____
Name

_____
Date

Don't miss the GOALS section at the end of this journal, starting on page 71.

Copyright © 2018 Sweet Harmony Press

All rights reserved. No part of this book may be reproduced or redistributed without express permission from the author and publishing company.

All graphic images are used with permission and the appropriate commercial use licenses.

Find more journals at

www.sweetharmonypress.com

Practice Notes

Practice Date	Place	Coach
Skills Practiced	Things to Remember	

Practice Date	Place	Coach
Skills Practiced	Things to Remember	

Practice Notes

Practice Date	Place	Coach
Skills Practiced	Things to Remember	

Practice Date	Place	Coach
Skills Practiced	Things to Remember	

Practice Notes

Practice Date	Place	Coach
Skills Practiced	Things to Remember	

Practice Date	Place	Coach
Skills Practiced	Things to Remember	

Practice Notes

Practice Date	Place	Coach
Skills Practiced	Things to Remember	

Practice Date	Place	Coach
Skills Practiced	Things to Remember	

Practice Notes

Practice Date	Place	Coach
Skills Practiced	Things to Remember	

Practice Date	Place	Coach
Skills Practiced	Things to Remember	

Practice Notes

Practice Date	Place	Coach
Skills Practiced	Things to Remember	

Practice Date	Place	Coach
Skills Practiced	Things to Remember	

Practice Notes

Practice Date	Place	Coach
Skills Practiced	Things to Remember	

Practice Date	Place	Coach
Skills Practiced	Things to Remember	

Practice Notes

Practice Date	Place	Coach
Skills Practiced	Things to Remember	

Practice Date	Place	Coach
Skills Practiced	Things to Remember	

Practice Notes

Practice Date	Place	Coach
Skills Practiced	Things to Remember	

Practice Date	Place	Coach
Skills Practiced	Things to Remember	

Practice Notes

Practice Date	Place	Coach
Skills Practiced	Things to Remember	

Practice Date	Place	Coach
Skills Practiced	Things to Remember	

Practice Notes

Practice Date	Place	Coach
Skills Practiced	Things to Remember	

Practice Date	Place	Coach
Skills Practiced	Things to Remember	

Practice Notes

Practice Date	Place	Coach
Skills Practiced	Things to Remember	

Practice Date	Place	Coach
Skills Practiced	Things to Remember	

Practice Notes

Practice Date	Place	Coach
Skills Practiced	Things to Remember	

Practice Date	Place	Coach
Skills Practiced	Things to Remember	

Practice Notes

Practice Date	Place	Coach
Skills Practiced	Things to Remember	

Practice Date	Place	Coach
Skills Practiced	Things to Remember	

Practice Notes

Practice Date	Place	Coach
Skills Practiced	Things to Remember	

Practice Date	Place	Coach
Skills Practiced	Things to Remember	

Practice Notes

Practice Date	Place	Coach
Skills Practiced	Things to Remember	

Practice Date	Place	Coach
Skills Practiced	Things to Remember	

Practice Notes

Practice Date	Place	Coach
Skills Practiced	Things to Remember	

Practice Date	Place	Coach
Skills Practiced	Things to Remember	

Practice Notes

Practice Date	Place	Coach
Skills Practiced	Things to Remember	

Practice Date	Place	Coach
Skills Practiced	Things to Remember	

Practice Notes

Practice Date	Place	Coach
Skills Practiced	Things to Remember	

Practice Date	Place	Coach
Skills Practiced	Things to Remember	

Practice Notes

Practice Date	Place	Coach
Skills Practiced	Things to Remember	

Practice Date	Place	Coach
Skills Practiced	Things to Remember	

Practice Notes

Practice Date	Place	Coach
Skills Practiced	Things to Remember	

Practice Date	Place	Coach
Skills Practiced	Things to Remember	

Practice Notes

Practice Date	Place	Coach
Skills Practiced	Things to Remember	

Practice Date	Place	Coach
Skills Practiced	Things to Remember	

Practice Notes

Practice Date	Place	Coach
Skills Practiced	Things to Remember	

Practice Date	Place	Coach
Skills Practiced	Things to Remember	

Practice Notes

Practice Date	Place	Coach
Skills Practiced	Things to Remember	

Practice Date	Place	Coach
Skills Practiced	Things to Remember	

Practice Notes

Practice Date	Place	Coach
Skills Practiced	Things to Remember	

Practice Date	Place	Coach
Skills Practiced	Things to Remember	

Practice Notes

Practice Date	Place	Coach
Skills Practiced	Things to Remember	

Practice Date	Place	Coach
Skills Practiced	Things to Remember	

Practice Notes

Practice Date	Place	Coach
Skills Practiced	Things to Remember	

Practice Date	Place	Coach
Skills Practiced	Things to Remember	

Practice Notes

Practice Date	Place	Coach
Skills Practiced	Things to Remember	

Practice Date	Place	Coach
Skills Practiced	Things to Remember	

Practice Notes

Practice Date	Place	Coach
Skills Practiced	Things to Remember	

Practice Date	Place	Coach
Skills Practiced	Things to Remember	

Practice Notes

Practice Date	Place	Coach
Skills Practiced	Things to Remember	

Practice Date	Place	Coach
Skills Practiced	Things to Remember	

Practice Notes

Practice Date	Place	Coach
Skills Practiced	Things to Remember	

Practice Date	Place	Coach
Skills Practiced	Things to Remember	

Practice Notes

Practice Date	Place	Coach
Skills Practiced	Things to Remember	

Practice Date	Place	Coach
Skills Practiced	Things to Remember	

Practice Notes

Practice Date	Place	Coach
Skills Practiced	Things to Remember	

Practice Date	Place	Coach
Skills Practiced	Things to Remember	

Practice Notes

Practice Date	Place	Coach
Skills Practiced	Things to Remember	

Practice Date	Place	Coach
Skills Practiced	Things to Remember	

Practice Notes

Practice Date	Place	Coach
Skills Practiced	Things to Remember	

Practice Date	Place	Coach
Skills Practiced	Things to Remember	

Practice Notes

Practice Date	Place	Coach
Skills Practiced	Things to Remember	

Practice Date	Place	Coach
Skills Practiced	Things to Remember	

Practice Notes

Practice Date	Place	Coach
Skills Practiced	Things to Remember	

Practice Date	Place	Coach
Skills Practiced	Things to Remember	

Practice Notes

Practice Date	Place	Coach
Skills Practiced	Things to Remember	

Practice Date	Place	Coach
Skills Practiced	Things to Remember	

Practice Notes

Practice Date	Place	Coach
Skills Practiced	Things to Remember	

Practice Date	Place	Coach
Skills Practiced	Things to Remember	

Practice Notes

Practice Date	Place	Coach
Skills Practiced	Things to Remember	

Practice Date	Place	Coach
Skills Practiced	Things to Remember	

Practice Notes

Practice Date	Place	Coach
Skills Practiced	Things to Remember	

Practice Date	Place	Coach
Skills Practiced	Things to Remember	

Practice Notes

Practice Date	Place	Coach
Skills Practiced	Things to Remember	

Practice Date	Place	Coach
Skills Practiced	Things to Remember	

Practice Notes

Practice Date	Place	Coach
Skills Practiced	Things to Remember	

Practice Date	Place	Coach
Skills Practiced	Things to Remember	

Practice Notes

Practice Date	Place	Coach
Skills Practiced	Things to Remember	

Practice Date	Place	Coach
Skills Practiced	Things to Remember	

Practice Notes

Practice Date	Place	Coach
Skills Practiced	Things to Remember	

Practice Date	Place	Coach
Skills Practiced	Things to Remember	

Practice Notes

Practice Date	Place	Coach
Skills Practiced	Things to Remember	

Practice Date	Place	Coach
Skills Practiced	Things to Remember	

Practice Notes

Practice Date	Place	Coach
Skills Practiced	Things to Remember	

Practice Date	Place	Coach
Skills Practiced	Things to Remember	

Practice Notes

Practice Date	Place	Coach
Skills Practiced	Things to Remember	

Practice Date	Place	Coach
Skills Practiced	Things to Remember	

Practice Notes

Practice Date	Place	Coach
Skills Practiced	Things to Remember	

Practice Date	Place	Coach
Skills Practiced	Things to Remember	

Practice Notes

Practice Date	Place	Coach
Skills Practiced	Things to Remember	

Practice Date	Place	Coach
Skills Practiced	Things to Remember	

Practice Notes

Practice Date	Place	Coach
Skills Practiced	Things to Remember	

Practice Date	Place	Coach
Skills Practiced	Things to Remember	

Practice Notes

Practice Date	Place	Coach
Skills Practiced	Things to Remember	

Practice Date	Place	Coach
Skills Practiced	Things to Remember	

Practice Notes

Practice Date	Place	Coach
Skills Practiced	Things to Remember	

Practice Date	Place	Coach
Skills Practiced	Things to Remember	

Practice Notes

Practice Date	Place	Coach
Skills Practiced	Things to Remember	

Practice Date	Place	Coach
Skills Practiced	Things to Remember	

Practice Notes

Practice Date	Place	Coach
Skills Practiced	Things to Remember	

Practice Date	Place	Coach
Skills Practiced	Things to Remember	

Practice Notes

Practice Date	Place	Coach
Skills Practiced	Things to Remember	

Practice Date	Place	Coach
Skills Practiced	Things to Remember	

Practice Notes

Practice Date	Place	Coach
Skills Practiced	Things to Remember	

Practice Date	Place	Coach
Skills Practiced	Things to Remember	

Practice Notes

Practice Date	Place	Coach
Skills Practiced	Things to Remember	

Practice Date	Place	Coach
Skills Practiced	Things to Remember	

Practice Notes

Practice Date	Place	Coach
Skills Practiced	Things to Remember	

Practice Date	Place	Coach
Skills Practiced	Things to Remember	

Practice Notes

Practice Date	Place	Coach
Skills Practiced	Things to Remember	

Practice Date	Place	Coach
Skills Practiced	Things to Remember	

Practice Notes

Practice Date	Place	Coach
Skills Practiced	Things to Remember	|//

Practice Date	Place	Coach
Skills Practiced	Things to Remember	

Practice Notes

Practice Date	Place	Coach
Skills Practiced	Things to Remember	

Practice Date	Place	Coach
Skills Practiced	Things to Remember	

Practice Notes

Practice Date	Place	Coach
Skills Practiced	Things to Remember	

Practice Date	Place	Coach
Skills Practiced	Things to Remember	

Practice Notes

Practice Date	Place	Coach
Skills Practiced	Things to Remember	

Practice Date	Place	Coach
Skills Practiced	Things to Remember	

Practice Notes

Practice Date	Place	Coach
Skills Practiced	Things to Remember	

Practice Date	Place	Coach
Skills Practiced	Things to Remember	

Practice Notes

Practice Date	Place	Coach
Skills Practiced	Things to Remember	

Practice Date	Place	Coach
Skills Practiced	Things to Remember	

Practice Notes

Practice Date	Place	Coach
Skills Practiced	Things to Remember	

Practice Date	Place	Coach
Skills Practiced	Things to Remember	

Practice Notes

Practice Date	Place	Coach
Skills Practiced	Things to Remember	

Practice Date	Place	Coach
Skills Practiced	Things to Remember	

Goals

Date Goal Set	Target Date to Achieve Goal	Date Goal Achieved
My Goal:	What I Need to Do to Achieve This Goal	

Date Goal Set	Target Date to Achieve Goal	Date Goal Achieved
My Goal:	What I Need to Do to Achieve This Goal	

Date Goal Set	Target Date to Achieve Goal	Date Goal Achieved
My Goal:	What I Need to Do to Achieve This Goal	

Date Goal Set	Target Date to Achieve Goal	Date Goal Achieved
My Goal:	What I Need to Do to Achieve This Goal	

Goals

Date Goal Set	Target Date to Achieve Goal	Date Goal Achieved
My Goal:	What I Need to Do to Achieve This Goal	

Date Goal Set	Target Date to Achieve Goal	Date Goal Achieved
My Goal:	What I Need to Do to Achieve This Goal	

Date Goal Set	Target Date to Achieve Goal	Date Goal Achieved
My Goal:	What I Need to Do to Achieve This Goal	

Date Goal Set	Target Date to Achieve Goal	Date Goal Achieved
My Goal:	What I Need to Do to Achieve This Goal	

Goals

Date Goal Set	Target Date to Achieve Goal	Date Goal Achieved
My Goal:	What I Need to Do to Achieve This Goal	

Date Goal Set	Target Date to Achieve Goal	Date Goal Achieved
My Goal:	What I Need to Do to Achieve This Goal	

Date Goal Set	Target Date to Achieve Goal	Date Goal Achieved
My Goal:	What I Need to Do to Achieve This Goal	

Date Goal Set	Target Date to Achieve Goal	Date Goal Achieved
My Goal:	What I Need to Do to Achieve This Goal	

Goals

Date Goal Set	Target Date to Achieve Goal	Date Goal Achieved
My Goal:	What I Need to Do to Achieve This Goal	

Date Goal Set	Target Date to Achieve Goal	Date Goal Achieved
My Goal:	What I Need to Do to Achieve This Goal	

Date Goal Set	Target Date to Achieve Goal	Date Goal Achieved
My Goal:	What I Need to Do to Achieve This Goal	

Date Goal Set	Target Date to Achieve Goal	Date Goal Achieved
My Goal:	What I Need to Do to Achieve This Goal	

Goals

Date Goal Set	Target Date to Achieve Goal	Date Goal Achieved
My Goal:	What I Need to Do to Achieve This Goal	

Date Goal Set	Target Date to Achieve Goal	Date Goal Achieved
My Goal:	What I Need to Do to Achieve This Goal	

Date Goal Set	Target Date to Achieve Goal	Date Goal Achieved
My Goal:	What I Need to Do to Achieve This Goal	

Date Goal Set	Target Date to Achieve Goal	Date Goal Achieved
My Goal:	What I Need to Do to Achieve This Goal	

Goals

Date Goal Set	Target Date to Achieve Goal	Date Goal Achieved
My Goal:	What I Need to Do to Achieve This Goal	

Date Goal Set	Target Date to Achieve Goal	Date Goal Achieved
My Goal:	What I Need to Do to Achieve This Goal	

Date Goal Set	Target Date to Achieve Goal	Date Goal Achieved
My Goal:	What I Need to Do to Achieve This Goal	

Date Goal Set	Target Date to Achieve Goal	Date Goal Achieved
My Goal:	What I Need to Do to Achieve This Goal	

Goals

Date Goal Set	Target Date to Achieve Goal	Date Goal Achieved
My Goal:	What I Need to Do to Achieve This Goal	

Date Goal Set	Target Date to Achieve Goal	Date Goal Achieved
My Goal:	What I Need to Do to Achieve This Goal	

Date Goal Set	Target Date to Achieve Goal	Date Goal Achieved
My Goal:	What I Need to Do to Achieve This Goal	

Date Goal Set	Target Date to Achieve Goal	Date Goal Achieved
My Goal:	What I Need to Do to Achieve This Goal	

Goals

Date Goal Set	Target Date to Achieve Goal	Date Goal Achieved
My Goal:	What I Need to Do to Achieve This Goal	

Date Goal Set	Target Date to Achieve Goal	Date Goal Achieved
My Goal:	What I Need to Do to Achieve This Goal	

Date Goal Set	Target Date to Achieve Goal	Date Goal Achieved
My Goal:	What I Need to Do to Achieve This Goal	

Date Goal Set	Target Date to Achieve Goal	Date Goal Achieved
My Goal:	What I Need to Do to Achieve This Goal	

Made in the USA
Columbia, SC
20 April 2025